Anonymus

Constitution of the Most Worthy Grand, Worthy Grand, County, Primary and Juvenile Lodges of the British Templars

Anonymus

Constitution of the Most Worthy Grand, Worthy Grand, County, Primary and Juvenile Lodges of the British Templars

ISBN/EAN: 9783741184437

Manufactured in Europe, USA, Canada, Australia, Japa

Cover: Foto ©Lupo / pixelio.de

Manufactured and distributed by brebook publishing software (www.brebook.com)

Anonymus

Constitution of the Most Worthy Grand, Worthy Grand, County, Primary and Juvenile Lodges of the British Templars

CONSTITUTION

OF

THE MOST WORTHY GRAND, WORTHY GRAND, COUNTY, PRIMARY, AND JUVENILE LODGES

OF

THE BRITISH TEMPLARS.

BY-LAWS OF

...... *Perseverance* Primary Lodge, No. *165*

County of ...... *Grey* ......

Province of Ontario.

1871.

DECLARATION.

We, who are designated " British Templars, " in regular session convened, and intending, under God's blessing and guidance, to consider and determine upon all such matters as shall appear necessary for the welfare of our Society, desire in the first place, for the avoiding of all misunderstanding, to make a solemn declaration of the principles upon which we propose to proceed. Feeling that it is both natural and reasonable that those who have common rights to protect, common interests to defend, and common objects to obtain, should act together and know each other, we have resolved to form an Association for the protection of ourselves and our fellow beings from the many evils of Intemperance—for the securing of mutual assistance when needed—and for the elevation of our intellectual and moral characters ; and being aware that through want of that organization which secures concentrated effort, the benevolent objects of Patriots and Christians are often frustrated, and the best and noblest exertions for the public weal defeated ; we declare our firm and unanimous resolution, in dependence on Divine aid, to preserve those principles ourselves, to facilitate and promote their acquirement and dissemination, and to transmit them unimpaired to posterity ; and we do hereby pledge ourselves, with a view to secure more effectually the needed organization, to be governed by the following Constitution and Laws.

FAITH, HOPE, CHARITY.

British Templars!

PROVINCE OF ONTARIO.

This is to Certify that

M~ *John Fleming*

was this *30th* day of *February*

18*75*, duly admitted a Member of

Perseverance Lodge, N̊ ..

located in *Liberty*

Ontario

In witness whereof, see the signature of our Worthy
Chief Templar and Worthy Secretary.

.... *W. C. T.*

.... *W. Secy.*

GENERAL RULES.

1. The title of the Society is " *The British Templars.* "

2. The Order shall consist of an unlimited number of members, whose admission must be regulated in strict accordance with the requirements of the Order.

3. There shall be five grades of Lodges in the government of the Order, viz. :—Most Worthy Grand, Worthy Grand, Worthy County, Primary, and Juvenile.

4. Primary Lodges shall be permitted to give three Degrees, namely—Heart, Charity, and Royal Virtue.

5. The Charters, Rituals, Cermonies, Constitutions, Cards, Insignia and Emblems, used by the Lodges and members of the Order, shall be such, and none other, as are recognized by and received from the M. W. G. Lodge, through the W. Grand Secretaries.

6. Each Worthy Grand, Worthy County, Primary, and Juvenile Lodge may make rules for the good government of its proceedings, provided that such rules are not contrary to the Constitution and General Rules of the Order; and all members of such Lodges are bound to obey them.

7. A member or visitor, on entering a Primary Lodge, must invariably give to the Outer Guard the Quarterly Password, and to the Inner Guard the explanation thereof; and then walk up to the centre of the hall, face the Brother fill ing the chair of the W. Past Chief, and give the working sign of the Lodge; and after it is acknowledged by the W. Past Chief, the Brother may take his seat. In entering a Degree meeting, the party seeking admission, must give the Quarterly Password, with its explanation, to the Outer Guard, the Password of the Degree that is in working, to the Inner Guard; and, on entering the Lodge, the sign of the Degree to the W. Past Chief, who shall acknowledge it by the coun-

tersign. Persons seeking admisson to a County, a W. Grand. or to Most Worthy Grand Lodge, must give first the Quarterly Password and its explanation to the W. Outer Guard; secondly, the password of the County, Grand, or M. W. G. Lodge, as the case may be, to the W. Inner Guard; and thirdly, the sign of the Lodge to the W. Past Chief, who shall acknowledge it by the countersign; after which, the party may take his seat.

8. No decoration appertaining to the Order, shall be worn in any Lodge, unless the member wearing it be strictly entitled to it, either by virtue of the office he fills, or in consequence of being a member of a Lodge of which the decoration worn is an emblem.

9. Any person wishing to speak, shall rise and address the W. Chief of the Lodge, whom he shall address by the title of Most Worthy Grand, Worthy Grand, Worthy County, or Worthy, as the case may be. When a brother and sister rise at the same time, the sister shall have the floor; but if two brothers or two sisters (or more than two) rise at once, the Chief shall name the one who shall speak first; and no member shall be improperly interrupted while speaking.

10. Any member called to order, shall immediately sit down, unless permitted to explain.

11. When the Chief is putting a question, no member shall leave the Lodge, or walk across the hall.

12. Each member of a Lodge, who is entitled to a vote, and who is present when a question is put to the Lodge, shall vote thereon, if requested by five members, unless excused by a majority vote of the Lodge.

13. The yeas and nays upon any vote, shall be recorded in the minutes of any Lodge, when demanded by five members of the Lodge in which the vote is being taken.

14. Any Lodge may, by a unanimous vote, pass a resolution to take all votes by a show of hands, and dispense with ballots.

15. In the election of officers, a majority of all the votes present shall be necessary to a choice. The name having the lowest number of votes shall each time be withdrawn; and in case of a tie between the last two, the presiding officer shall give the casting vote. Two or more names may be withdrawn at a time, provided the lowest one remaining increased by the whole number of votes struck off, will not equal the highest.

16. When a vacancy occurs in any office, the Lodge in which the vacancy occurs, may fill the same at a regular meeting, provided that the claims of the Constitution are all complied with. And the person elected to fill the vacancy, shall be entitled to all the honors of the office.

17. All Past Chiefs who are elected at the institution of Lodges, shall retain the honors thereof, as if they had passed through the Chair.

18. In case of absence of an officer of any Lodge, the Worthy Chief of that Lodge shall appoint a brother or sister to fill, *pro tem.*, the vacant place. And in the absence of the Worthy Chief and Vice, the senior Past Worthy Chief Templar shall take the chair.

19. The Officers of any Lodge in the Order may be publicly installed, provided that a vote of two-thirds of the Lodge is favorable thereto.

20. No Provincial Deputy shall be entitled to exercise any of the functions of his office, after the Primary Lodge of which he is a member ceases to work constitutionally, or a successor to him has been appointed.

21. Representatives from any Lodge in the Order shall, if they demand it prior to their appointment as Representatives, be paid their actual pecuniary expenses.

22. All members of the higher grades of Lodges, who attend all sessions of each, shall be entitled to a copy of the Report of the session, provided that it is published.

23. At all meetings of the higher grades of Lodges, it shall

be determined before the close, when and where the next
meeting shall be held.

24. The first six Officers, together with the last Past Chief,
shall constitute the Executive Council of the M. W. Grand,
W. Grand, and W. County Lodges, respectively, to act in the
interval between their sessions; but the W. Chief and W.
Secretary shall be the Executive Officers for the transaction
of business, when neither the Lodge nor the Executive Council thereof is in session.

25. The Passwords shall be communicated by the Password Committee of the M. W. G. Lodge to the M. W. G.
Chief; and if approved by him, he shall have them forwarded to each of the W. G. Chiefs, who shall, through their W.
G. Secretaries, give the Password for each quarter, as it becomes due to each of the W. County Secretaries under the
jurisdiction, to be transmitted to the Provincial Deputy of
each Primary Lodge in the County—provided that the Password shall not in any case be given to any Lodge or member in default of dues: nor shall any Officer or a Representative be allowed to speak or vote in any Lodge, unless the
Primary Lodge of which he is a member shall have previously paid all its dues.

26. All fees received for Initiation and for Degrees, shall
be paid to the treasury of the Lodge of which the candidate
is a member.

27. In Primary Lodges, no candidate can be initiated except in open Lodge; and no Lodge can be opened without
a Charter, or certificate for Charter, signed by the proper
Officers.

28. Application for Charter shall be made according to the
form in the Appendix, by seven or more persons in good
standing in the community, through an Executive Officer
of the M. W. Grand or W. Grand Lodge, or a Provincial
Deputy, to the Worthy Grand Lodge of the province or
country in which the Lodge is to be located.

29. The fee which shall accompany the application for each Charter for a Primary Lodge, shall be eight dollars ($8.00); four dollars ($4.00) of this price shall go to the organizing officer who opens the Lodge, and four dollars ($4.00) to the Worthy Grand Secretary, who shall pay two dollars ($2.00) thereof into the W. Grand Treasury, and send the remaining two dollars ($2.00) to the M. W. Grand Lodge.

30. Each Primary Lodge Charter shall bear the signatures of the M. W. G. Chief, and M. W. G. Secretary, and also those of the W. G. Chief and W. G. Secretary of the W. G. Lodge under which the Lodge granted the Charter is to work.

31. Applications for Charters for Primary Lodges, from any Province or country in which no W. Grand Lodge exists, shall be made to the M. W. Grand Lodge direct; and such Primary Lodges shall make their returns and pay their dues directly to the M. W. Grand Secretary, until a W. Grand Lodge is formed in that Province or country.

32. Any member who shall at any time make known to any person who is not a member of the Order, in good standing, or to any member not entitled to receive it, any matter or thing connected with the secret working of the Order, shall be deemed guilty of a violation of the obligation of the Order, and shall be fined, suspended, expelled, or otherwise dealt with, according to the judgment of the Lodge whose obligation the member may have violated.

33. Any dispute or question of order, not otherwise provided for, shall be decided by the W. Chief of the Lodge in which it occurs, but always subject to an appeal to the Lodge, if demanded in writing by five members. In all cases where a member considers himself aggrieved by the decision of any Lodge, he shall have a right to appeal to the next highest tribunal of the Order—*exempli gratia*, from the Juvenile Lodge to the Primary Lodge to which it belongs; from the Primary to the County; then to the W. G. Lodge; and lastly to the M. W. G. Lodge, whose decision shall be final; provided that

County Lodges shall be the final arbiter in appeals arising in Juvenile Lodges.

34. When an appeal has been made, all the documents and Minutes relating to the matter in despute, shall be transmitted to the next highest tribunal; and all decisions made by any Lodge, shall be considered final, unless specially appealed from within one month after judgment is given.

35. All grades of Lodges shall be subject to those Lodges higher in authority, in matters not inconsistent with the Constitution. But no Lodge of the Order is obliged to recognize, or act on, any business or document sent them, unless it is properly authenticated.

36. No person can be a member of more than one Primary Lodge at the same time.

37. In the practical application of the Rules of this Order, the construction put upon them by the M. W. G. Lodge shall be final and conclusive. Every word in the singular number shall be applicable to the plural, and every word importing the masculine gender shall, when necessary, be understood to refer to a sister as well as a brother, and *vice versa*, unless there is something in the subject matter or context repugnant to such construction.

CONSTITUTION

OF THE

Most Worthy Grand Lodge.

ARTICLE 1.—NAME AND EXTENT.

There shall be a M. W. G. Lodge for the whole of the British dominions, to be called the "Most Worthy Grand Lodge of the British Templars."

ART. 2.—POWER.

The Most Worthy Grand Lodge is not only the sole depositary and guardian of the Symbols and Mysteries of the Order, but also the source of supreme legislation for the good government, uniformity, and general management of the Institution, and the final arbiter in all matters of dispute. It alone shall have power to alter or amend the Constitutions, Rituals, Ceremonies, Insignia, Forms, Signs, Passwords, Symbols, Mysteries, or Lectures; to originate the Quarterly and other Passwords; to fix the per centage to be paid by the Worthy Grand Lodges to it: to order what Regalia shall be worn by the Officers and members of the different grades of Lodges in the Order; but no alteration shall be made without a two-thirds vote taken on a notice of motion given at a previous Annual Session of the M. W. G. Lodge, unless recommended by a Worthy Grand Lodge, when the alteration may be made during the session at which said communication is received.

ART 3.—OF WHOM COMPOSED.

That the M. W. G. Lodge may contain only those who bring with them that measure of wisdom in council, combined with that zeal and experience in action, which shall lead to more glorious triumphs on the part of our noble Order—therefore the M. W. G. Lodge shall consist of its own officers, all the officers of each of the W. G. Lodges, all Past M. W. G. Chiefs, and all Past M. W. G. Secretaries, in good standing in the Order, all Provincial Deputies, all County Chiefs, a Representative from each County Lodge, together with a Representative for every ten Primary Lodges in good standing, under the jurisdiction of each of the W. G. Lodges, who shall have been elected at the regular annual session of the W. G. Lodges. These Representatives shall have

taken all the degrees, and shall have passed the chair of the W. Chief
or the W. Vice in a Primary Lodge.

ART. 4.—OFFICERS.

The Officers of the M. W. G. Lodge shall be a—

Most Worthy Grand Chief Templar,
"   "   Vice,
"   "   Secretary,
"   "   Treasurer.
"   "   Lecturer,
"   "   Counsellor,
"   "   Chaplain,
"   "   Financier,
"   "   Recorder,
"   "   Marshal,
"   "   Deputy Marshal,
"   "   Inner Guard,
"   "   Outer Guard,
"   "   Past Chief,

who, with the exception of the M. W. G. Past Chief, shall be e'ected at
a regular annual session of the M. W. G. Lodge, and shall serve one
year. Any member of the M. W. G. Lodge, in good standing, shall be
eligible, if present.

ART. 5.—DUTIES OF OFFICERS.

SEC. 1.—The M. W. G. C. T. shall preside in the M. W. Grand Lodge,
decide all questions of usage, as well as constitutional questions, subject to an appeal to the M. W. Grand Lodge. He shall have power to
visit W. Grand Lodges personally or by Deputy, and require a compli-
ance with the rules and usages of the Order ; or he may require from
any W. G. C. T. any necessary information relative to his W. Grand
Lodge. He shall see that all officers and committees not otherwise
provided for are duly appointed; cause to be sent to the W. Grand
Lodges all the general Passwords of the Order; have power to grant
Charters for Primary Lodges in Provinces or Countries in which no W.
Grand Lodge exists, as well as for W. Grand Lodges, when proper application has been made by the W. C. T.'s of at least seven Primary
Lodges in each Province or Country. All Charters so granted shall be
subject to the approval of the M. W. Grand Lodge, at its first regular
session following. He shall make such arrangements for the proper
opening of the Lodges authorized by him, as in his judgment circum-
stances may demand.

SEC. 2.—The M. W. G. Vice shall assist the M. W. G. Chief; and in
his absence, preside in his stead. The M. W. G. Vice shall have im-

mediate charge of general matters relating to the ingress and egress of members and visitors.

SEC. 3.—The M. W. G. Sec'y shall be the custodian of the Great Seals of the Order, the Charters, Rituals, Books, Papers, Correspondence, and other property of the M. W. Grand Lodge. He shall attend all meetings of the M. W. Grand Lodge, and see that a correct record of the proceedings is kept, conduct the correspondence under the direction of the M. W. G. Chief, keep true accounts between the M. W. Grand Lodge and the Lodges under its jurisdiction, receive all moneys due the M. W. Grand Lodge, and pay the same to the M. W. Grand Treasurer. He shall perform such other duties connected with his office as may be enjoined upon him by the Executive, or by the M. W. Grand Lodge ; and at each annual session of the M. W. Grand Lodge, he shall present a written statistical report. He shall give security for the faithful performance of his duty, in a bond to the M. W. G. Chief, the M. W. G. Vice, and the M. W. G. Past Chief, in the penal sum of Five Thousand Dollars ($5.000), with two good and sufficient sureties, and shall be entered into before installation ; and receive for his services such compensation as the M. W. Grand Lodge may from time to time determine by open vote.

SEC. 4.—The M. W. G. Treasurer shall have charge of the funds, securities, and vouchers of the M. W. G. Lodge ; pay all orders drawn on him by the M. W. G. Secretary, attested by the M. W. Grand Chief ; at each meeting of the M. W. Grand Lodge, produce his books of account, with proper vouchers, for examination and audit ; he shall, before installation, give security for the faithful discharge of his duty, in a bond to the M. W. G. C. T., M. W. G. V. T., and P. M. W. G. C. T., in the penal sum of Five Thousand Dollars ($5.000), with two good and sufficient sureties ; and when going out of office, deliver up to his successor all the property of the M. W. Grand Lodge in his possession.

SEC. 5.—The M. W. G. Lecturer shall be the Right Hand Supporter of the M. W. G. Chief ; and when so directed by the Executive of the Order, he shall travel through the country to give public Lectures on the Order, and the Temperance Cause in general. He shall visit Lodges, and explain the unwritten work of the Order, and by his counsel in Lodges, and his addresses at Public Meetings, strive to promote the objects of the Order.

SEC. 6.—The M. W. G. Counsellor shall be the Left Hand Supporter of the M. W. G. Chief. He shall be the guardian of the rights and liberties of the Subordinate Lodges, and of the members of the M. W. Grand Lodge. He will assist the M. W. G. Chief in presiding, and in his temporary absence fill his chair and discharge his duties ; and if he omit any part of his duty, the M. W. G. Counsellor will remind him of it.

SEC. 7.—The M. W. G. Chaplain shall conduct the religious part of the opening and closing solemnities, and the other religious services of the M. W. Grand Lodge.

SEC. 8.—The M. W. G. Financier shall examine the Books of the M. W. G. Secretary and M. W. G. Treasurer, and present an Annual Statement of the Financial condition of the Order; recommend to the M. W. Grand Lodge the amount of Per Capita Tax he may deem it expedient for the M. W. G. Lodge to levy from year to year; and see that the names of all sisters and brothers who attend the M. W. G. Lodge are recorded in their own hand writing in a book which shall be kept for that purpose, together with the name and number of their Lodges, and the capacity in which each one is present.

SEC. 9.—The M. W. G. Recorder shall faithfully record in the Journal of the M. W. G. Lodge, all the transactions of each session of the M. W. G. Lodge, and he will also aid the M. W. G. Secretary as he may from time to time require.

SEC. 10.—The M. W. G. Marshal, assisted, when necessary, by the M. W. G. Deputy Marshal, shall introduce the Representatives and Visitors for obligation, and the M. W. Grand Officers for installation; arrange the furniture, &c., of the Lodge Room; tell the votes; and have charge of all matters relating to the insignia and regalia to be worn by the officers and members of the M. W. Grand Lodge. He shall also manage all processions and public services of the M. W. Grand Lodge, and have charge of all that relates to cavalcades, soirees, &c.

SEC. 11.—The M. W. G. Deputy Marshal shall introduce the Lady Representatives and Visitors, and have charge of matters relating to the insignia and regalia of the sisters in the M. W. Grand Lodge.

SEC. 12.—The M. W. G. Inner Guard shall have charge of the inner door of the M. W. G. Lodge, and shall not allow a member or visitor to enter or retire without the proper Password, unless directed by the M. W. G. Chief, Vice, or Lodge.

SEC. 13.—The M. W. G. Outer Guard shall have charge of the outer door and ante-rooms, and allow none to enter but those duly authorized.

SEC. 14.—The M. W. G. Past Chief shall by his superior experience and intelligence, aid the M. W. G. Officers in the discharge of their duties, attend the meetings of the Executive Council of the Order, and shall continue, with unabated devotion and undiminished zeal, to guard and advance the interests of the Temperance cause and of our excellent Institution.

ART. VI.—ORDER OF BUSINESS.

Opening of M. W. Grand Lodge.
Appointment of Committee on Credentials.
3 Report.
4 Reading Minutes of last Session, (short.)
5 Fixing Hours of Meeting.
6 Appointment of Committees on Juvenile Lodges;—Making Lodges more Attractive, Profitable and Stable;—Memorials;—Correspondence;—Appeals;—State of the Order;—Passwords;—Constitutional Changes, &c. &c. &c.
7 Receiving Reports of M. W. G. Chief; –Secretary;—Treasurer; —Lecturer;—and Financier.
8 Receiving Reports of Committees appointed at last Session to Report at present one.
9 Unfinished Business.
10 Receiving Reports of Committees.
11 New Business.
12 Fixing Time and place of next Session.
13 Election of Officers.
14 Installation.
15 Closing.

[NOTE.—The Minutes of each Sitting to be read immediately after the opening ceremonies of the following one.]

ART. 7.—DEPUTIES.

The M. W. Grand Lodge, or its Executive, shall have power to appoint one or more Deputy M. W. G. Chief Templars for any Province or Country having no W. Grand Lodge; and the Deputies thus appointed shall organize Lodges and exercise a general supervision of the Order in such Province or country until the organization of a W. Grand Lodge therein.

ART. 8.—DUES AND RETURNS.

The Per Capita Tax and returns shall be forwarded quarterly by each W. Grand Secretary, to the M. W. G. Secretary, with all possible promptness, after the form provided by the M. W. Grand Lodge, stating the number of County, Primary, and Juvenile Lodges in the jurisdiction—the names of Provincial Deputies—the number of members admitted, withdrawn, suspended, expelled, died, violated the pledge, and reinstated, during the term—the number of brothers and sisters respectively—the whole amount of money on hand—the names and P. O. addresses of all Representatives to the M. W. Grand Lodge within the jurisdiction of each W. G. Lodge. No Worthy Grand Lodge, whose dues and returns have not been sent to the M. W. Grand Lodge, shall be entitled to receive the Passwords, or to have a voice or vote in the M. W. Grand Lodge, except by a two-thirds vote of the members present.

ART. 9.—REVENUE.

The M. W. Grand Lodge shall derive its revenue from the following sources :—Twelve dollars ($12) for each W. Grand Lodge Charter; two dollars ($2) for each Primary Lodge Charter—a sum not exceeding one cent *per capita*, quarterly, on the membership under the jurisdiction of each of the W. Grand Lodges—and the profits arising from the sale of stock at ten (10) per cent. premium,

ART. 10.—REGALIA.

The Regalia to be worn in the Most Worthy Grand Lodge, shall be Royal Purple Velvet Collars, trimmed with Gold Lace and Bullion Fringe, and faced, for officers and members, on the left, with a bronze or silver British Coat of Arms. For Officers, on the right, there shall be silver Emblems, as follows :

M. W. G. Chief—All seeing Eye.
    "   Vice—Gavel.
    "   Secretary—Cross Pens.
    "   Treasurer— "   Keys.
    "   Lecturer—Star.
    "   Counsellor—Inverted Wine Cup.
    "   Chaplain—Open Bible.
    "   Financier—Single Key.
    "   Recorder—Single Pen.
    "   Marshal—Cross Staves.
    ."   Deputy Marshal—Single Staff.
    "   Inner Guard—Sword.
    "   Outer Guard—Cross Swords.
    "   Past Chief— "   Gavels.

For members, on the right, gold or silver Star.

ART. 11.—VOTING.

In voting for Officers, each member of the M. W. Grand Lodge shall have one vote. On ordinary questions, the vote may be taken as per usage; but when demanded by at least three members from different W. Grand Lodges, it shall be taken by W. Grand Lodges, the M. W. G. Secretary shall call the W. Grand Lodges, according to the date of their organization, and a majority of Representatives present shall govern the vote. If the Representatives of a Province be equally divided the vote shall be lost. In voting by W. Grand Lodges, each W. Grand Lodge shall have one vote for the first five hundred members, or less. under its jurisdiction, and one additional vote for every additional five hundred, up to five thousand, and one additional vote for every one thousand above that number.

ART. 12.—QUORUM.

That twenty (20) members, representing at least a majority of the Worthy Grand Lodges, shall be a quorum for the transaction of business; but a smaller number may open the Lodge, and receive reports,

ART. 13.—WORKING DEGREE.

The M. W. Grand Lodge shall be opened in the highest Degree of the Order, and hold all its sessions under its working; and all members of the Order who have been duly exalted to this Degree, and are clothed in proper regalia, can be present at its sessions, by taking the necessary obligations.

ART. 14.—PUNISHMENT FOR CONTUMACIOUSNESS.

The Executive Officers of any Worthy Grand Lodge refusing or neglecting to enforce or comply with the Constitution, precedents, usages and ceremonies ordained by the Most Worthy Grand Lodge, shall forfeit their position; and the Charter and property of such W. Grand Lodge shall be taken charge of in the meantime by the M. W. G. Chief and M. W. G. Secretary, who shall exercise the powers entrusted to them until other officers are duly elected to perform the duties of the W. G. Lodge.

ART. 15.—W. G. L. CONSTITUTION.

The Most Worthy Grand Lodge ordains and establishes the following as the Constitution of Worthy Grand Lodges; and any W. Grand Lodge neglecting or refusing to comply with the Rules and regulations therein contained, shall forfeit its Charter and other property,

G. LODGE OF ONTARIO, BRITISH TEMPLARS, IV ···ORG'D NOVEMB'R 18, 1868···

CONSTITUTION

OF

WORTHY GRAND LODGES.

~~~~~~~~~~~~~~~~~~~~~~~

ART. 1—*Number of Primary Lodges required for the Establishment of a Worthy Grand Lodge.*

That as soon as five (5) Primary Lodges are organized in any Province. Colony, or Dependency of the British Empire, or in any of the three principal Divisions of the Kingdom of Great Britain and Ireland, that Province, Colony, Dependency, or Division, shall be entitled to organize a W. Grand Lodge, on the same plan, and having the same powers and privileges as those W. Grand Lodges already constituted.

ART. 2—*Name.*

This Worthy Grand Lodge shall be known as "The Worthy Grand Lodge of the British Templars of ———."

ART. 3—*Power.*

Worthy Grand Lodges shall have power to divide their own territory into Counties, fix the amount of *per capita tax* to be levied on Primary Lodges within their jurisdiction, rescind or confirm decisions of County Lodges, regulate their own Provincial business, and make such rules for their government, and the government of the Lodges and members under their jurisdiction, as they may deem necessary, and as shall not conflict with the sovereignty of the M. W. Grand Lodge, or the Constitution of the Order, as enacted and interpreted by the M. W. Grand Lodge, or as shall not be in violation of the laws of the land.

ART. 4—Of Whom Composed.

The W. G. Lodges shall be composed of their own officers;
the officers and past Chiefs and past Secretaries of the M.
W. G. Lodge, who belong to Primary Lodges within the Province or Country; all past W. G. Chiefs, and past W. G. Secretaries in good standing in the jurisdiction; their W. County Chiefs and W. County Secretaries, and a Representative
for every five (5) Primary Lodges in the County; all com-
missioned Provincial Deputies, together with a Representative from each Primary Lodge for every thirty (30) members. All these Representatives must be elected from present and past Chiefs and Vice.

ART. 5—Officers.

The W. Grand Officers shall be—Chief Templar, Vice, Secretary, Treasurer, Lecturer, Counsellor, Chaplain, Financier.
Recorder, Marshal, Deputy Marshal, Inner Guard, Outer
Guard, and Past Chief; each having the title " Worthy
Grand" prefixed. All these, except the W. G. Past Chief,
shall be elected at the Annual Session, and serve one year;
and any member of the W. G. Lodge in good standing shall
be eligible, if present. The W. G. Secretary, before installation, shall give security for the faithful performance of his
duty, in a bond to the W. G. C. T., W. G. V. T., and P. W.
G. C. T., in the penal sum of Four Thousand Dollars ($4,000),
with two good and sufficient sureties. The W. G. Treasurer,
before installation, shall give security for the faithful performance of his duty, in a bond to the W. G. C. T., W. G. V. T.,
and P. W. G. C. T., in the penal sum of Four Thousand Dollars ($4,000), with two good and sufficient sureties.

ART. 6—Duties of Officers.

The W. G. Lodge Officers shall discharge the same duties
in their respective W. G. Lodges as do the Officers of the M.
W. G. Lodge (mutatis mutandis). The W. G. Chiefs and W.
G. Secretaries shall also see that the Quarterly Returns and

per capita tax are forwarded in accordance with Articles 8 and 9 of the M. W. G. Lodge Constitution.

ART. 7—*Order of Business.*

The Order of Business shall be the same as that observed in the M. W. G. Lodge.

ART. 8—*Provincial Deputies.*

Each Primary Lodge shall, as often as necessary, elect and recommend to the W. G. C. T., as the Provincial Deputy for the Lodge, a member, in good standing, who shall have attained the full age of twenty-one years. If the appointment is approved, the W. G. Chief Templar shall grant the Brother a Provincial Deputy's Commission, signed by the W. G. C. T. and W. G. Secretary, which shall remain in force so long as the Brother continues a member of the Lodge, or until sufficient cause be shown for its revocation. In addition to the ordinary duties and privileges of a Provincial Deputy as laid down in his Commission, it shall be his special duty to instal the Officers of his Primary Lodge, to receive the quarterly and other passwords from the County, W. Grand, or M. W. Grand Secretary, and communicate them to the W. C. T. of his Lodge, and to see that the quarterly returns are properly made out, and the *per capita tax* paid previous to installation; and he shall immediately forward them (*i. e.*, returns and per capita tax) to the County Secretary, if a County Lodge exists there—if not, to the Worthy Grand Secretary; and in case there is no W. G. Lodge, direct to the M. W. Grand Secretary.

ART. 9—*Revenue.*

The Revenue of W. Grand Lodges shall be derived from the following sources : Four dollars ($4) for each Primary, and one dollar ($1) for each Juvenile Charter (and the property accompanying the same) granted to new Lodges within the Province, the capitation tax fixed at each Annual W. G. Lodge Session, to be paid by each Primary Lodge under its control; and the profits arising from the sale of its stock.

ART. 10.—Property to be sent with Primary Charter.

The W. G. Secretary shall send with each Charter granted to open a Primary Lodge, two (2) Primary Rituals, three (3) Rituals of each Degree, six (6) Constitutions, six (6) Return Sheets, one Key to Passwords, one Provincial Deputy's Commission, twelve (12) Odes, one set Officers' Cards, twelve (12) Blank Propositions, twelve (12) Blank Orders on Treasurer, twelve (12) Blank Financier's Receipts, &c.

ART. 11.—Property to be sent with Juvenile Charter.

The W. G. Secretary shall send with the Charter to each Juvenile Lodge, four (4) Rituals, six (6) Constitutions, twelve (12) Odes, twelve (12) Cards of membership, &c. &c.

ART. 12.—Regalia.

The Regalia to be worn by officers and members of the W. Grand Lodges, shall be Scarlet or Crimson Collars, trimmed with silver lace; and for officers, silver fringe in addition. The facing on the left, a silver star; on the right, for officers, the same emblems as for the M. W. Grand Lodge; for members, on the right, plain.

ART. 13.—Voting.

Unless otherwise demanded the vote on any question may be taken as per usage; but when the Representatives of two (2) County Lodges require it, the vote shall be taken by Lodges. When a vote by Lodges is demanded, the W. G. Secretary shall call the roll of County Lodges alphabetically, and the roll of Primary Lodges by number, beginging with number one, and a majoity of the Representatives present from each Lodge, shall govern the vote of the Lodge. If the Representatives of any Lodge are equally divided, the vote of that Lodge shall not be counted. In voting by Lodges, each County Lodge shall be entitled to one vote for every ten Primary Lodges under its jurisdiction; and each Primary Lodge shall be entitled to one vote for the first thirty members, or under, and to one additional vote for every

thirty members over the first thirty; and the officers of W,
G. Lodges shall each be entitled to one vote.

ART. 14.—*Quorum.*

To form a quorum for the transaction of business in W,
Grand Lodges, there shall be present not less than twelve
members, representing at least one County and five Prim,
ary Lodges.

ART. 15.—*Working Degree.*

The W. Grand Lodge shall open and hold all its sessions
under the second Degree of the Order; and all members
who have been duly raised to that Degree, and are clothed
in proper regalia, can be present at its sessions, after taking
the necessary obligations.

CONSTITUTION

OF THE

Worthy County Lodges.

ART. 1.—*Formation.*

As soon as there are three Primary Lodges in good standing in any County, or Parliamentary Division of a County, the Senior Provincial Deputy in the County shall by notice to the W. C. T. of each Primary Lodge in the County, call a meeting at such time and place as he may deem most convenient, for the purpose of organizing a County Lodge. If a majority of the Representatives present deem it necessary to organize a County Lodge, the said Provincial Deputy shall preside at such meeting until the County Officers have been elected, and the County C. T. installed, who then shall instal the other Officers of the County Lodge. In Counties where there are less than three Primary Lodges, those Lodges may unite for County purposes, with the adjoining County which may be most convenient, and make returns and pay dues through such County Lodge, and receive the quarterly Password from such County Secretary. Lodges, when not so united, shall make their returns to, and receive the quarterly Password from the W. Grand Secretary direct.

ART. 2.—*Name.*

Worthy County Lodges shall always bear the name of the County or Parliamentary Division of the County in which the Primary Lodges constituting the Worthy County Lodge are located.

ART. 3.—Powers.

A County Lodge shall have the power to adjudicate on any appeals from the decisions of Primary Lodges, or of Provincial Deputies belonging to Lodges in the County; to settle disputes arising between two or more Primary Lodges; to send its Chief or Lecturer to visit Primary Lodges, for the purpose of delivering public lectures on the Order, or on the principles of temperance; of redressing grievances arising in Primary Lodges, and of doing all the acts necessary to promote the interests of the Order in the County over which it presides.

ART. 4.—How Composed.

A County Lodge shall be composed of the M. W. Grand Officers and W. Grand Officers, including all Past M. W. G. and W. G. Chiefs and Secretaries, in connection in the County, its own Officers, all its own Past Chiefs and Past Secretaries in good standing in the Order, the Provincial Deputy, the Degree Templar, and the Officers of each Primary Lodge in the County, who have taken the first Degree, together with a Representative from each Primary and Juvenile Lodge, for every thirty (30) members, elected on the night of installation each term.

ART. 5.—Sessions.

County Lodges shall hold their regular Quarterly Sessions in the months of December, March, June, and September—the June Session being considered the Annual.

ART. 6.—Officers.

The Officers of the W. County Lodges shall be (mutatis mutandis) the same in number, name, duties and privileges respectively, in connection with their County Lodges, as the Officers of the W. Grand Lodges. The W. County Treasurer, before installation, shall give security for the faithful performance of his duty, in a bond to the W. Co. C. T., W. Co. V. T., and P. W. Co. C. T., in the penal sum of Two Hundred Dollars ($200), with two good and sufficient sureties.

ART. 7.—Worthy County Chief.

The W. County Chief, besides his ordinary duties, shall cause the County Secretary to make out and forward to the W. Grand Secretary, immediately after the June meeting of the County Lodge, a list of all such Provincial Deputies as are certified by the different Primary Lodges to be in full and regular standing in the Order; and this list shall bear the Seal of the County Lodge and the signatures of the County Chief and County Secretary.

ART. 8.—Worthy County Secretary.

The W. County Secretary, in addition to the other duties of his office, shall within ten days after the close of each session of the W. County Lodge, send to the W. Grand Secretary a full and true account of all the business done therein. The W. Co. Secretary, before installation, shall give security for the faithful performance of his duty, in a bond to the W. Co. C. T., W. Co. V. T., and P. W. Co. C. T., in the penal sum of Four Hundred Dollars ($400), with good and sufficient sureties.

ART. 9.—Election of Officers and Representatives.

The County Officers shall be elected annually at the June Session; and Representatives to the M. W. Grand and W. Grand Lodges annually at the session immediately preceding the sessions of those bodies respectively.

ART. 10.—Order of Business.

The Order of Business shall be the same (as near as may be) as that observed in the M. W. Grand Lodge.

ART. 11.—Fees.

The County Lodge shall receive one cent of the capitation tax per quarter for each and every member of the Primary Lodges in connection therewith, to be sent by the Provincial Deputy of each Primary Lodge, with the Quarterly Returns and other dues, to the County Secretary,

who shall pay over the County Allowance to the County Treasurer; and Primary Lodges shall not receive the Password
until this rule is complied with. County Lodges shall have
power to exact dues from Juvenile Lodges, if they think
proper to impose them.

ART. 12.—Regalia.

The Regalia worn in the W. County Lodges shall be Blue
Collars, decorated in such a manner as may be decided upon by the members, provided there is borne upon the face
something that will show connection with our British Templars, and not encroach upon the higher grades of Regalia.

ART. 13.—Quorum.

Seven members, representing at least two Primary Lodges,
shall constitute a quorum for the transaction of business.

ART. 14.—Working Degree.

The County Lodge shall open and hold all its sessions in
the first Degree; and those who have received that Degree,
and are clothed in proper regalia. can be present at its
meetings; and shall enroll their name as required in the
higher grades of Lodges.

ART. 15.—Dormant Lodges.

When any Primary Lodge is suspended, surrenders its
Charter, or becomes dormant from any cause whatever,
the Charter, Rituals, Books, Funds, &c., and other property of the dormant Lodge, shall be taken into possession by the County Chief, in the name and on behalf
of the County Lodge; and any claims against the dormant Lodge, which do not amount to over one-half the value
of the property received, shall be paid from the County
fund ; and any locality in the same County may, by constitutionally applying for the said property, for the purpose of
opening a Lodge, and by paying two-thirds of the original
costs, receive the same, taking also the name and standing

in priority of the dormant Lodge; provided always that upon the application of seven or more members of an extinct Lodge to the County Lodge, for the restoration of such Lodge to fellowship, accompanied with satisfactory evidence that a fair opportunity has been given to all that were members in good standing at the time the Lodge ceased working, to unite in such application, they may be restored to fellowship in said Lodge, together with the Charter and effects of said Lodge, taken possession of by the County Lodge. Any Primary Lodge failing to hold meetings for six months, or to make returns, as required by the Constitution, for one year, shall be deemed a dormant Lodge, and its Charter shall be forfeited.

CONSTITUTION

OF THE

PRIMARY LODGES.

Article 1.—Name.

This Lodge shall be styled *~~Terrores~~ ~~Pr~~*imary Lodge, No. *16.5* of "British Templars," in the County of *Grey*, and ~~~~ of *Derby*

Article 2.—How Constituted.

This Lodge shall consist of not less than seven members, four of whom, viz., the Provincial Deputy, the Degree Templar, the W. C. T., and the Worthy Vice, shall be eligible and they only shall receive all the Degrees; and the remaining Officers, being of proper age, shall receive the first Degree.* None of its members shall be less than fourteen years of age; and all shall have subscribed to the following pledge.

Article 3.—Pledge.

No member shall make, buy, sell, use, or give, as a beverage, any spirituous or malt liquors, wine, cider, or other intoxicating drinks; but each shall, in all proper ways, discountenance the manufacture and sale thereof.

---

* Officers, elected at the *formation* of a Lodge, are entitled to receive the Degrees, as mentioned in this Article, FREE OF CHARGE.—*Journal M. W. G. L., Session of* 1869, pp. 11, 12.

Article 4.—*Charter*.

This Lodge shall hold an unforfeited Charter from the W. G. Lodge, signed in accordance with Section 30, General Rules; and it cannot voluntarily surrender its Charter, unless two weeks' notice has been previously given in open Lodge, of the intention so to do, or even then, if seven members object thereto.

Article 5.—*Membership*.

Sec. 1—The name and residence of a person offered for membership must be in writing; and the proposition, made by a member of the Lodge, with two referees, must be entered on the records, and the subject referred to three members for investigation ; two of whom shall be appointed by the W. C. T., and the third by the W. V. T. The Committee shall report in writing at the next regular meeting. All candidates must be ballotted for with ball ballots ; and if not more than four black balls appear, the applicant shall be declared elected ; but if more than four appear, or if all the ballots cast be black, he shall be rejected, and so declared. But no member shall mention a person proposed for membership, to any one, except a member of the Lodge, until after the decision has been given, and not even then, if the candidate has been rejected. No person so rejected shall be again proposed or initiated in any Lodge of the Order, under three months, unless by the unanimous vote of the Lodge.

Sec. 2—A proposition for membership shall not be withdrawn after it has been referred to a Committee for investigation, without the consent of a majority of the members present.

Sec. 3—No suspended member of the Order, can be received in membership in any Lodge, except on being reinstated and receiving a card of clearance from the Lodge which suspended him. A member suspended for non-payment of dues, may be reinstated by paying the dues standing against him at the time of his suspension.

Sec. 4—The character of a candidate for membership may be discussed in the Lodge any time after the report of the Investigating Committee is presented, and previous to the ballot being taken; but it is improper to call on any member for the reasons of his vote.

Sec. 5—The name of any person applying for membership by deposit of Card, shall be subject to the same proposition, investigation, and ballot, as a new applicant, and on being admitted shall sign the Constitution of the Order, and obligations of the Degrees taken, (if any,) and retain all unforfeited honors previously gained.

Sec. 6—A candidate may be proposed, ballotted for, and initiated at any regular meeting, by the unanimous consent of the members present; in which case, the Investigating Committee shall report at the same meeting in which the candidate is proposed.

Sec. 7—Any candidate after being proposed and elected, who does not appear within one month for initiation, must be again ballotted for before he is admitted. And applicants for a Charter, who do not appear within three months after the organization of the Lodge, shall be subject to the same regulations as new candidates.

Article 6.—Officers.

Sec. 1—The Officers of a Primary Lodge shall be—Worthy Chief Templar, Worthy Vice Templar, Secretary, Treasurer, Chaplain, Financier, Marshal, Inner Guard, Outer Guard, (elective,) Right Hand Supporter, Left Hand Supporter, Assistant Secretary, Deputy Marshal, (appointed,) and the Past Worthy Chief (for the most part,) *ex officio.*

Sec. 2—After a Lodge has been instituted three full terms, no member shall be eligible to the office of W. C. T., or W. V. T., unless he has served a regular term in some subordinate office, either elective or appointed; and has taken, previous to nomination, all the Degrees given in a Primary Lodge.

Sec. 3—All Officers must be clear of any charges on the books before being installed ; and any member in good standing shall be eligible for office, except as provided in the previous section.

Sec. 4—The Officers, except as otherwise provided, shall be nominated and elected at the last regular meeting in each term, and installed at the first regular meeting in the succeeding term.

Sec. 5—Any Officer failing to appear for installation at the time provided for in section 4 of this article, or absenting himself for three successive meetings, the seat may be declared vacant by a two-thirds vote of the members present, unless a satisfactory excuse for absence be given.

Sec. 6—In case the seat of any Officer becomes vacant, such vacancy shall be filled at any regular meeting ; and any member who shall fill the vacancy for the remainder of the quarter, shall be entitled to the full honors of the term.

Article 7.—Duties of Officers.

Sec. 1—It shall be the duty of the W. C. T. to preside in the Lodge, enforce a due observance of the Constitution, rules and usages of the Order; see that all Officers and Committees perform their respective duties ; appoint all officers and committees not otherwise provided for; give the casting vote on all matters before the Lodge, when a tie shall occur ; inspect and announce the result of all balloting and other votes; direct the Secretary to call special meetings when application in writing shall have been made by five members of the Lodge; and draw on the Treasurer for all sums necessary to pay the appropriations made by the Lodge. He shall, on the night he vacates the chair, see that the quarterly returns are carefully and properly prepared for the County Lodge and W. Grand Lodge, duly certified by him with the Seal of the Lodge attached ; and also that all Grand Lodge and County dues are paid to the Installing Officer. He shall perform such other duties as the Lodge or his charge may require.

Sec. 2.—It shall be the duty of the W. V. T. to render the W. C. T. such assistance as may be required of him ; and in the absence of the W. C. T., to perform his duty.

Sec. 3.—The Secretary shall keep a fair and impartial record of the proceedings of the Lodge, write communications, fill certificates, summon meetings when ordered by the Worthy Chief, attest all moneys ordered to be paid at a regular meeting, and none other ; inform any Lodge of the deposit in his Lodge of a Clearance Card granted by the former; and notify all Primary Lodges not more than five miles from its place of meeting, within one week after, of the name and residence of every person rejected, withdrawn, suspended or expelled from his Lodge. He will be parti- cular to write words, names and figures plainly; he will at- tach the seal of his Lodge to all returns, credentials, and official communications; and see that no writing is placed on the back or face of the credentials or returns, but such as properly belongs to them. In remitting moneys he will state distinctly how they are to be appropriated; and in all his official communications with the W. County or the W. G. Lodge, he will be careful to state the name and number of his own Lodge, its Post Office address, and the County to which it is attached. At the end of his term, previous to the installation of officers, he shall make out for the Lodge a full report of the proceedings of the term, and he is strict- ly charged to have the Quarterly Return Sheet neatly, fully, and correctly prepared on the day of installation. He shall enter in the Minute Book of his Lodge a synopsis of the re- turns sent to the W. County or the W. Grand Secretary; and he shall perform such other duties as may be required of him by the Lodge or his charge, and deliver up to his successor within one week from the expiration of his term, all books, papers, and other property of the Lodge that may be in his possession.

Sec. 4.—It shall be the duty of the Treasurer to give his bond of not less than....dollars, with such surety as may be approved by the Lodge; to pay all orders drawn on him by the W. C. T., attested by the Secretary, and none other. He shall receive all moneys of the Lodge, and hold the same until the expiration of his term, unless otherwise ordered by the Lodge. He shall keep a full and correct account of all moneys received and expended; and at the end of his term previous to the installation of officers, he shall present a report of the same. He shall perform such other duties as may be required by the Lodge or his charge; and at the expiration of his term, or when legally called upon to do so, deliver up all moneys, books, papers, vouchers and other Lodge property in his possession to his successor in office, or the person appointed to receive the same.

Sec. 5.—It shall be the duty of the Chaplain to perform the religious solemnities of the Lodge.

Sec. 6.—It shall be the duty of the Financier to keep just and true accounts between the Lodge and its members, credit the amounts paid, and pay the same over to the Treasurer immediately, taking his receipts therefor. At the end of his term, previous to the installation of officers, he shall make out for the Lodge a full report, and furnish the Secretary with the amount of receipts, initiation fees and dues, during his term, together with the initiation fees for the Degrees, with any other information connected with his office necessary to enable the Secretary to prepare correct returns for the County and Grand Lodge. He shall perform such other duties as the Lodge or his charge may require of him; and at the expiration of his term, deliver up to his successor all property appertaining to his office in his possession.

Sec. 7.—It shall be the duty of the Marshal to introduce for initiation persons who have been previously elected; also the Grand Lodge Officers and other distinguished visitors. He shall examine the brothers present at the opening of the Lodge in the Quarterly Password and the explanation, and report to the W. C. T. any that are not in possession of them. He shall see that the officers' and members' Regalia, the

Ode and other Cards, and the Books are in their proper places at the opening of the Lodge, and he shall take charge of the same at the close. He shall tell the votes when required, and have charge of such property of the Lodge as may not otherwise be provided for.

Sec. 8.—It shall be the duty of the Inner Guard to attend the door of the Hall, and to admit no one who is unable to give the explanation of the Quarterly Password, unless by special direction of the Lodge. Candidates for initiation under charge of the Marshal are to be admitted to the Lodge Room. The Inner Guard shall not permit egress to any one without his giving the retiring Password received from the Deputy Marshal, except as elsewhere specially provided.

Sec. 9.—The Outer Guard shall not permit any one to pass him without the reception of the Quarterly Password, or the direction of the Lodge, except candidates for admission to the Lodge. He shall keep off all intruders, have charge of the ante-rooms, and see that the order of the Lodge is not disturbed by any annoyances therein.

Sec. 10.—The R. and L. Hand Supporters shall discharge the duties laid down in their installation charges.

Sec. 11.—The Assistant Secretary shall call the roll of Officers, note the absentees, and announce those absent at the last meeting. He shall see that each member on joining the Lodge sign the Constitution; and he shall keep in a proper place in the roll-book a list of all those withdrawn, suspended, expelled, or violated pledge, &c., giving the time, and other needed information. He shall also render to the Secretary such assistance as may be required.

Sec. 12.—It shall be the duty of the Deputy Marshal to examine the sisters present at the opening of the Lodge, in the Quarterly Password and Explanation, and report to the W. C. T. any that are not in possession of them; and render such other services as the Marshal or the Lodge may require.

Article 8.—Degrees.

Sec. 1.—Members who are sixteen (16) years of age, and

upwards, have been in membership three (3) months, and have conducted themselves in such a manner as to be worthy of advancement, may take the first Degree; and when eighteen (18), and upwards, the second and third Degrees.

Sec. 2.—At least one month shall elapse between the conferring of each Degree, except as provided in Article 2; and no member shall receive a Degree, except in the Lodge to which he belongs, unless by a written permission from his Provincial Deputy.

Sec. 3.—Members wishing advancement. must apply for the same at the proper time, in a regular meeting of the Primary Lodge, paying the Financier the fee, and taking his receipt; and any Degree member may, when the Lodge is open in the appropriate Degree, lay the names with the receipts, of the candidates before the Lodge, when they shall be ballotted for the same as persons seeking ordinary membership; provided always, that if rejected, the application fee be refunded.

Sec. 4.—Each Primary Lodge shall have a Degree Templar elected annually at the first meeting in February; and he shall ordinarily be the presiding officer of the Degree Meeting in his own Lodge, confer the Degrees, and in the absence of the Provincial Deputy, or other higher official in the Order, he shall perform in his own Lodge the Provincial Deputy's ordinary duties; provided always, he be not by virtue of his office a member of any higher grade of Lodge than that of County.

Sec. 5.—The proceedings of the Degree Meetings shall be recorded in a separate book kept for the purpose.

Article 9.—Fees and Dues.

The Initiation fee in Primary Lodges (except for clergymen, and as hereinafter provided) shall be not less than fifty cents ($0.50) for brothers, and twenty-five cents ($0.25) for sisters. The fee for each degree shall be twenty-five cents ($0.25). Each Lodge shall regulate its Weekly or Quarterly Dues so as to meet the expenditure, the Dues being paid in advance, and no member shall be entitled to receive the Password unless he is clear on the books of the Financier. Persons in destitute circumstances may be admitted without initiation fees or dues, by the unanimous vote of the Lodge.

Article 10.—*Returns.*

At the end of each Quarter every Primary Lodge shall, through its Provincial Deputy, report to the County and Grand Lodge the working of the Quarter, according to the form provided by the M. W. G. Lodge, accompanied by the capitation tax for the quarter; provided that where no County Lodge exists, the return shall be made direct to the W. Grand Secretary; and where there is no W. Grand Lodge, direct to the M. W. G. Secretary.

Article 11.—*Terms.*

The regular quarterly terms shall commence on the first day of November, February, May, and August, and any Primary Lodge refusing or neglecting to make returns for one year, or failing to hold meetings for six months, shall forfeit its charter.

Article 12.—*Representatives.*

Each Primary Lodge shall elect at the first meeting in February, from the present and past Chiefs and Vices, one Representative to the W. Grand Lodge for every thirty (30) members; and also, on the night of installation in each quarter, one Representative to the County Lodge for every thirty (30) members; provided, however, that the Lodge shall have power to supply the place of any that may be disqualified or unable to attend. Any Lodge having less than thirty (30) members shall be entitled to send one Representative.

Article 13.—*Cards.*

Sec. 1.—A Card of clearance shall be granted and used when a member wishes to leave his Lodge to join another Lodge, and it shall be available for the length of time a member pays his dues, but it shall not exceed six months from the date thereof.

Sec. 2.—A Travelling Card shall be granted and used when a member is about to go on a journey, on his paying all dues in advance for the full time such Card is desired, not exceeding one year, and the fee for the Card.

Sec. 3.—Application for either Travelling or Clearance Cards must be made in open Lodge, at a regular meeting thereof. The Card shall be granted by a vote of the Lodge, provided there is no charge pending against the applicant, and that he is clear on the Financier's Books, and pays the necessary dues and the fee for the Card.

Sec. 4.—Persons holding Travelling or Clearance Cards continue to be members of the Order, and are amenable to all the laws of their respective Lodges in the same manner as other members; but when a Card has expired by limitation, the holder of it can make application to his own Lodge for membership as if the time had not expired; yet a person cannot be admitted as a visitor to a Lodge, or to membership in a strange Lodge on an expired Card.

Sec. 5.—Travelling and Clearance Cards must bear the Seal of the Order, be signed by the W. Chief, and attested by the Secretary, under the seal of the Primary Lodge granting the Card. The name of the holder must be written in the margin in his own handwriting, and the name of the W. Grand Secretary must also be on the Card.

Sec. 6.—Any member applying for a Travelling or Clearance Card, may withdraw the application at any time before the Card is actually granted.

Article 14.— Withdrawals.

A member in good standing may withdraw from the Order by making written application, provided he is clear of any charges on the Books of the Financier.

Article 15.— Visiting Members.

No member can visit in any Lodge without he is in possession of the Password and Explanation for the current Quarter without the permission of the Lodge, unless he pre-

ınexpired Travelling Card, and proves him·
·elling Password. On presentation of the
, the Provincial Deputy shall proceed to ex-
)r in the Travelling Password and Signs, the
ing. If the Prov. Deputy, is satisfied with the
ımination, he will introduce the visitor with-
ımony. In case of the absence of the Prov.
ber who has received the three Degrees shall
perform the duty. A Lodge shall have the
admittance to a visiting member who can
pon being satisfied that he has lost his mem·
ı irregularly admitted, or has previously de·
mproperly in the Lodge.

Article 16.—*Offences.*

nember of a Primary Lodge who shall violate
. be deprived of all official honors previous·
shall not be eligible for office sooner than
fter.

member, who has good reasons to believe
·r of the Order has violated his pledge or ob·
ıstitution or Laws, or has in any way been
:t unbecoming a British Templar, shall pre·
inst him according to the form in the appen·
itution, within one month after knowledge
:ommitted, has come to him.

member accused of any offence against this
entitled to and shall receive a fair trial. No
ı placed on trial for any offence except the
made out in writing, and signed by a member
d the party accused shall be put in possession
harges and specifications, and have a full and
e of the place and time of meeting, at least
·us to the trial.

nember against whom an act of violation of
een brought in open Lodge, shall be notifi·
e Secretary; and, if after a receipt of such

notice, the accused member, within seven days, shall not
appear at the Lodge and plead to the charge, or demand an
investigation thereof, the charges and specifications shall
be referred to a Committee of three members, in good standing in the Lodge, who shall report at its regular meeting,
when the case may be tried: and in all cases when practic-
able, the accused and the accuser shall be summoned before
the Committee, and be allowed counsel if they wish, provided they (the counsel) are members of good standing in the
Order.

Sec. 5.—All testimony received by a Committee when investigating the charges against a member, should be reduced to writing, and read in the Lodge if required.

Sec. 6.—If the accused fail to appear when duly summoned, the Committee shall report him guilty of contempt and
this report, if adopted by the Lodge, shall be final, and the
W. C. T. shall, in two weeks thereafter, declare the member
expelled, unless it shall appear that the accused was unavoid-
ably absent; and in this case the accused shall be entitled
to a rehearing.

Sec. 7.—When any Committee report the charges sustained, and the report is adopted by the Lodge, the offending
party shall be fined, reprimanded, suspended, or expelled,
as the vote of the Lodge at any regular meeting may determine.

Sec. 8.—All votes for reinstatment or expulsion shall be by
ball ballot.

Sec. 9.—If the accused be not satisfied with the decision
of the Primary Lodge, appeal may be taken to the Provincial Deputy or to the County Lodge, the minutes and papers
being delivered therewith, and his decision or that of the
County Lodge shall be final, unless appealed from within
one month after judgment is given.

Sec. 10.—A member under charges, and during the investigation thereof by the Lodge, is in a state of suspension,

and cannot vote or speak on any question under consideration, unless by the permission of the Lodge.

Sec. 11.—Any brother who shall wilfully or maliciously bring charges against a member, and fail to prove the same, shall be fined, reprimanded, suspended, or expelled, as the Lodge may determine.

Sec. 12.—Any member having been expelled, shall not be again proposed for membership under three months from date of expulsion, unless by a two-thirds vote of the Lodge.

Sec. 13.—Any member six months in arrears, shall be notified of the same by the Financier of the Lodge, and if such arrears are not cancelled as the Lodge may direct, the member may be expelled by a vote of the Lodge at any regular meeting

Sec. 14.—When a member, accused of violating his obligation, shall be present and plead guilty to the charge, the case may be tried forthwith, without the appointment of a Committee ; but at the request of the accused, final action may be postponed one week.

Sec. 15.—Any person who shall be guilty of any objectionable or disorderly conduct, or disrespectful language in the Lodge, may be fined, reprimanded, suspended, or expelled, as the Lodge may determine by a majority vote taken by ball ballot, at the time the offence is committed, or at either of the next two subsequent meetings.

Sec. 16.—If a member acknowledge a violation of the pledge, the W. C. T. shall—1st, call the attention of the Lodge; 2d, rise from his seat ; 3d, declare that all the honors the said member (giving his name), had previously attained, are forfeited; 4th, take a ballot on the expulsion of the member, and if a majority present vote therefor, he shall declare the said member expelled, and order the Assistant Secretary to strike the name from the books, and make an entry of the cause for so doing. But if a majority do not vote for the expulsion, the membership of the offender shall bo retained, and no further action shall be taken, except that the Lodge may, by a majority vote, require the offender to be re-obligated. in the Primary and Degree obligations (the latter being applicable to Degree members only).

Sec. 17.—Should a member not come forward for re-obligation before one month, the W. C. T. shall declare the membership of the offender forfeited.

Article 17.—*Regalia.*

Sec. 1.—Primary Lodges may adopt any style of Regalia, provided the impress of British Templarism appears on the same, and if possible the name of the Lodge.

Sec. 2.—Officers' Regalia shall be Scarlet.

Sec. 3.—Degree Badges shall be purple, with rosette containing the emblematic colors of the Degrees taken,

Article 18.—*Quorum.*

Five members shall constitute a quorum for the transaction of business.

Article 19.—*By-Laws.*

Any Primary Lodge shall be at liberty to adopt such By-Laws, have order of business, and Regulations as may be deemed advisable; provided. however, that no By-Law or Regulation shall conflict with the Constitution, General Rules, or any part of the Rules of Order.

CONSTITUTION

OF

JUVENILE LODGES.

------◦------

Article 1.—Name.

This Lodge shall be styled.—— Juvenile Lodge, No. —— in the County of ——, and Province of ——, belonging to the British Templars.

Article 2.—Object.

The object shall be—To attach the rising generation to the Temperance Cause; to enlighten them upon the great principles of Total Abstinence—the necessity of its prevalence—and as a consequence, the suppression of the present drinking usages of society; to impress on them the great duty devolving upon them in regard to the future prospects of the Cause; and prepare them, by our mode of business, for the regular Lodges of the British Templars, or for other adult Temperance organizations.

Article 3.—Pledge.

SEC. 1.—I do solemnly and sincerely engage that, from this date, I will neither make, buy. sell, use, nor give, as a beverage, any spirituous or malt liquors, wine, cider, or other intoxicating drinks; and that I will discountenance their use in the community.

SEC. 2.—I further engage that I will not use Tobacco in any form; and that I will observe the Constitution, By-Laws, and Usages of the Brisish Juvenile Templars.

Sec. 3.—I also declare that, with God's help, I will not use profane or indecent language.

Article 4.—Officers.

Sec. 1.—There shall be four Adult and seven Juvenile Officers. The Adult Officers called respectively—Worthy Guardian, Associate Guardian, Chaplain, and Treasurer, must be members of, and appointed by, a regular Primary Lodge of British Templars, meeting at or near the place where the Juvenile Lodge assembles. The Juvenile Officers called respectively—Secretary, Financier, Marshal, Deputy Marshal, Assistant Secretary, Inner Guard and Outer Guard, are to be members of the Lodge.

Sec. 2.—The Adult and Juvenile Officers shall be nomin-ated and elected half yearly, at the last regular meetings in June and December ; and shall be installed by the Pro-vincial Deputy (or a person acting in that capacity,) at the next meeting following.

Article 5.—Duties of Officers

Sec. 1.—The Worthy Guardian, who, by virtue of office, is head of the Lodge, shall preside at all the ordinary meetings, and exercise a general control over the Lodge. He shall make such decisions, and impart such advice, as may be deemed necessary to carry out the principles of this organization ; and shall also provide persons to address the Lodge at stated periods, and shall endeavour to inter-est, instruct and please the Juvenile charge.

Sec. 2.—The Associate Guardian shall, on all occasions, assist the Worthy Guardian, support him in maintaining order, and in case of the absence of that officer, officiate in his place.

Sec. 3.—The Chaplain shall perform the sacred duties pertaining to his office.

Sec. 4.—The Secretary shall record the Minutes and other proceedings ; notify meetings when ordered by the

W. G. ; attest to all moneys ordered to be paid at a regular meeting, and none other ; and perform such other duties as may be required of him by the Worthy Guardian of the Lodge.

SEC, 5.—The Financier shall keep the accounts of the Loage, and prepare statements thereof for the use of the Lodge.

SEC. 6.—The Treasurer shall receive all moneys from' members and others ; keep proper accounts with the members ; announce at the close of each meeting the amount received, and pay accounts when properly signed. At the end of his term of office, he shall bring a statement, showing the receipts and expenditures during the term ; also, showing the balance in hand. He shall perform such other duties as the Worthy Guardian or the Lodge may require of him.

SEC. 7.—It shall be the duty of the Marshal to introduce candidates to receive the pledge, &c. ; and after the service is concluded, he shall show the new members to a seat. He shall take charge of all property of the Lodge not properly in the possession of the other officers, and under the direction of the Worthy Guardian, perform such other duties as may be required of him. He shall also introduce visitors, and lead them to their appointed seats.

SEC. 8.—It shall be the duty of the Deputy Marshal to render such service as the Marshal or the Lodge may require of him.

SEC. 9.—It shall be the duty of the Assistant Secretary to see that the Roll Book is neatly and properly kept ; and render the Secretary such assistance as he or the Lodge may require.

SEC. 10.—It shall be the duty of the Inner Guard to attend the door—to admit none but members of the Order, and candidates for initiation.

SEC. 11.—The Outer Guard shall guard the outside, and keep off intruders.

Article 6.—Membership.

SEC. 1.—No one under six years of age shall be admitted to membership in this Lodge ; but Juvenile Lodges have the power to decide at what age, over six, and under sixteen, persons may be admitted.

SEC. 2.—The entrance fee, to be determined by the Primary Lodge, shall not be less than five cents, or more than twenty.

SEC. 3.—No one shall be admitted to membership without the written consent of parent or guardian, unless on inquiry. sufficient cause exists for departing from this law; nor shall any one be admitted, or retained as a member, who uses profane language, or is addicted to gambling, cruel sports, or is indecent in conversation or manners.

SEC. 4.—All youths wishing to become members, must be proposed by a member of the Lodge, and duly elected, before being admitted as members. The proposer must state age, parentage, and residence, and must produce the certificate called for by Section 3 of this Article—when the candidate may be elected by a show of hands, for and against ; if six be against, he shall be declared rejected; if elected, the Worthy Guardian shall so declare.

SEC. 5.—Any member who shall be consistent for the space of at least twelve months previously, and is also clear on the books, both of dues and charges, shall, on being elected to membership in a Primary Lodge, have paid from the funds of the Juvenile Lodge of which he is a member, one half the initiation fee to said Primary Lodge.

Article 7.—Duties of Members.

Each member shall conscientiously observe the pledge, and shall, on all suitable occasions, advocate the cause of Total Abstinence; and shall use all lawful methods to bring proper youths into the Lodge. Members shall serve in office, and on committees, and perform such other reasonable duties as may be required of them; they shall not divulge the proceedings of the meetings to persons who are not members. They shall also show proper respect to the Worthy Guardian, Associate Guardian, Chaplain, and other officers of the Lodge.

Article 8.—Offence.

SEC. 1.—Any member violating Article 3. of the Constitution, or any other law, shall be reprimanded, fined, suspended, or expelled, as two-thirds present at any regular meeting may determine: if, upon investigation, the offence be proved.

SEC. 2.—Any officer violating the Constitution, By-Laws, or Rules of the Lodge, shall forfeit his office and honors, in addition to the penalty laid upon him by the 1st Section of this Article.

SEC. 3.—Charges against a member must be brought in writing, and the same handed to the Worthy Guardian, who shall, if there is evidence to sustain the charge, report the fact to the Lodge at the same or next meeting, with an order that the member be notified to appear before the Lodge for trial.

SEC. 4.—At the time of trial, the Worthy Guardian shall take the Chair, and act as Judge; and the evidence shall then be produced, when a two thirds majority of the members present shall decide upon the guilt or innocence of the accused, and the Worthy Guardian shall thereupon pass sentence accordingly, upon the accused member. It shall be in the power of a two-thirds majority to re-instate an expelled member, if they deem it well to do so, provided he pays a fine of 12½ cents. He must also re-sign the Constitution.

Article 9.—Regalia.

The Regalia for ordinary members shall be a badge of

the Order, on a sash or collar, as the Lodge may determine ;
and the Regalia for Officers shall be similar to that worn
by the Officers in the regular Lodge of British Templars.

Article 10.—Meetings.

This Lodge shall meet as often as may be convenient,
but not less frequently than once a month. The regular
times of meeting shall, when decided upon, be embodied
in the By-Laws.

Article 11.—Password.

There shall be a Quarterly Password for the Lodge. given
by the M. W. G. Chief, and no member of the Order shall
sit in the Lodge without giving it.

Article 12.—Adult Members.

An adult person upon becoming an Officer, and therefore
a member of a Juvenile Lodge, shall sign the Constitution
book, and become amenable to its laws. An adult person,
however, who objects to receive the clause in the Pledge
concerning Tobacco. can leave it out, and take the other
parts of the Pledge. It would be advisable, however, to
receive the Pledge entire.

Article 13.—Representation.

SEC. 1.—Each Lodge shall be entitled to send, for every
thirty members, one Representative to the meetings of the
W. County Lodge of the British Templars. Said Representatives to be one of the Adult Officers of the Lodge.

SEC. 2.—This Lodge shall, at the first regular meeting in
each quarter, ballot separately, and with ball ballots, for
Representatives to the County Lodge.

SEC. 3.—Each Representative of a Juvenile Lodge shall
be furnished with credentials of his appointment (signed by
the Secretary of the Juvenile Lodge.)

Article 14.—Funerals and Badges for them.

SEC. 1.—At the Funeral of a member, the Lodge will turn
out and march to the deceased member's house, and

thence (with the funeral cortege,) to the place of inter-
ment.

SEC. 2.—The Funeral Badge shall be a piece of crape
tied on *left arm.* The Lodge may, if desired, wear their
Regalia.

Article 15.—*Processions.*

SEC. 1.—A Juvenile Lodge walking in procession, shall
form as follows :—

Marshal.   Deputy Marshal.
Banner or Flag of the Lodge.
Chaplain.   Worthy Guardian.   Ass. Guard.
Past Worthy Guardian.
Treasurer.   Secretary.   Financier.
Inner Guard.   Ass't Secretary.   Outer Guard.
Members.
(Two or Four abreast.)
(*Other Flags may be carried also.*)

SEC. 2.—The Lodge shall march in advance of the
corpse, and on arriving at the ground, open right and left,
and remain uncovered, while the body and friends pass
through. The Banner or Flag shall be drooped at the same
time.

Article 16.—*The Gavel.*

It is recommended by the Grand Lodge that Lodges make
use of the "*Gavel.*" When it is used, there shall be a By-
Law to that effect: *one* rap calls to order and to be seated ;
two raps call up the Lodge.

Article 17.—*Reception of the W. G. C. T. or his Deputy.*

When the M. W., or W. G. C. T., or Deputy, pays a visit
to a Lodge, upon the fact being made known by the Marshal, the Worthy Guardian will call up the Lodge, the Marshal meanwhile leading the W. G. C. T., or Deputy to a

seat on the right of the Worthy Guardian ; while doing sc,
the Lodge will sing the following:

TUNE—"*Rosseau.*"
Welcome, Worthy of our Order,
Gladly we your entrance greet ;
Let our warmth, our friendly ardor,
Prove how happily we meet.
Such may all our meetings prove,
Each a brother, each a friend,
All our acts performed in love,
Good their aim, and peace their end,

(The Worthy Guardian will now call down.)

Article 18.—*Withdrawals, Cards, &c.*

SEC. 1.—Any member may withdraw from this Lodge, by
paying up his dues to the time of withdrawal, provided he
produces the written request or permission of parent or
Guardian, and is not under a charge, or one to be brought.

SEC. 2.—Upon withdrawing, a member, if he desires it,
may be presented with a Clearance Card, to run the length
of time his dues are paid in advance, not exceeding twelve
months from the date thereof, during which time said member may join any Juvenile Lodge of the Order, entrance free.

SEC. 3.—The Lodge shall present to every member, upon
joining, a Card of Membership.

Article 18.—*Quorum.*

Five members shall constitute a quorum for the transaction of business.

RULES OF ORDER.

DUTIES AND PRIVILEGES OF W. C. T.

1. It shall be the duty of the W. C. T. to preserve order, and endeavour to conduct all business before the Lodge to a speedy and proper result.

2. He shall state every question properly presented to the Lodge; and before putting it to vote, shall ask, "Is the Lodge ready for the question?" Should no member offer to speak, he shall rise to put it; and after he has risen, no member shall be permitted to speak upon it.

3. The W. C. T. shall have a casting vote in case of a tie; but in ordinary cases shall not vote. He shall announce all votes and decisions. His decisions on points of order shall not be debateable, unless, entertaining doubts on the subject, he invite discussion.

4. He may speak to points of order in preference to other members of the Lodge, rising from his seat for that purpose; and shall decide questions of order, subject to an appeal to the Lodge by five members, in writing. On such an appeal, no member shall speak more than once.

5. When an appeal is made from the decision of the W. C. T., he shall put the question thus: "Shall the decision of the Chair be sustained?"

6. It shall be the duty of the presiding Officer, and the privilege of any member of the Lodge, to call a member to order who violates an established rule of order.

MOTIONS.

7. A motion must be seconded, and afterwards repeated from the Chair, or read aloud, before it is debated. A motion shall be reduced to writing, if any member require it.

8. All resolutions shall be submitted in writing.

9. Any member having made a motion, may withdraw it, with leave of his seconder, before it is debated, but not afterwards, without leave of the Lodge.

10. A motion to amend an amendment to an amendment, sha'l not be entertained.

11. An amendment destroying or altering the intention of a motion, shall be in order ; but an amendment relating to a different subject, shall not be in order.

12. On an amendment to " strike out and insert," the paragraph to be amended, shall first be read as it stands : then the words proposed to be struck out and those to be inserted, and finally the paragraph as it would stand, if so amended.

13. On a call for a division on the question, the majority shall decide. The call can only be granted when the division called for will leave distinct and entire propositions.

DEBATE.

14. When a member speaks or offers a motion, he shall rise in his place, and respectfully address the W. C. T., confining himself to the question under consideration, and avoiding personality or unbecoming language.

15. When a member is called to order, he shall take his seat until the point is determined.

16. When two or more members rise to speak at the same time, the presiding officer shall decide who is entitled to the floor.

17. No member shall speak more than twice, or longer than five minutes, on any quest'on, without leave of the Lodge ; the same to be granted or refused without debate.

18. While a member is speaking, no one shall interrupt, except for the purpose of calling to order, or asking of the presiding officer leave to explain, or to call the previous question. A member allowed " to explain," shall only have a right to explain an actual misunderstanding of language, and shall be strictly prohibited from going into debate on the merits of the case.

19. For any member, in speaking, to impeach the motives of a fellow member, or treat him with personal disrespect, shall be deemed a violation of order, which may incur the censure of the presiding officer, or of the Lodge.

20. If any member shall feel personally aggrieved by a decision of the Chair, he may appeal from such decision.

21. Any conversation by whispering or otherwise, which is calculated to disturb a member while speaking, or hinder the transaction of

business, shall be deemed a violation of order ; and if persisted in, shall incur censure.

PRIVILEGED QUESTIONS.

22. When a question is before the Lodge, the only motions in order, shall be—1st, to adjourn ; 2nd, the previous question ; 3rd, to lay on the table ; 4th, to postpone indefinitely ; 5th, to postpone to a definite period ; 6th, to refer ; 7th, to divide, if the sense will admit of it ; or 8th, to amend : to take precedence as herein arranged, and the first three to be decided without debate.

23. When the previous question is moved and seconded, it shall be put in this form, "Shall the main question be now put ?" If this is carried, all further amendments and debate shall be excluded, and the question put without delay. If the question has been amended, the question shall be taken on the amendment first. If more than one amendment has been made, the last made amendment in order, shall take precedence in the vote. It shall not be in order to reconsider the agreement to take the previous question.

24. When a motion is postponed indefinitely, it shall not come up again during the session.

ADJOURNMENT.

25. A motion to adjourn shall always be in order, except—1st, when a member is in possession of the floor ; 2nd, while the yeas and nays are being called ; 3rd, when the members are voting ; 4th, when adjournment was the last preceding motion ; or 5th, when it has been decided that the previous question shall be taken.

26. A motion to adjourn cannot be amended ; but a motion to adjourn to a given time, may be, and is open to debate.

QUESTIONS NOT DEBATABLE.

27. 1st, A motion to adjourn, when to adjourn, simply ; 2nd, a motion to lay on the table, when claiming privilege over another motion ; 3rd, a motion for the previous question ; 4th, a motion to reconsider ; 5th, a motion to read a paper ; 6th, a motion to take up particular items of business ; 7th, questions of order, when not appealed from the decision of the W. C. T., or not submitted by him to the Lodge

READING OF PAPERS.

28. The reading of any paper called for, relating to the subject under debate, shall always be in order.

TAKING A VOTE.

29. When the presiding officer has commenced taking a vote, no further debate or remark shall be admitted, unless a mistake has been made ; in which case the mistake shall be rectified, and the presiding officer shall recommence taking the vote.

30. When the decision of any question is doubted, the presiding officer shall direct the Marshal to count the votes in the affirmative and negative, and report the same to him.

31. The yeas and nays upon any question before the Lodge, may be called for by two members ; and upon the assent of one-third of the members present, shall be taken. They may be called for at any time before a peremptory decision of the vote from the Chair.

32. In taking the yeas and nays, the S. shall call the roll, and record the yeas and nays ; after the roll is called, the result shall be read aloud, to rectify mistakes, (if any) ; after which, the S. shall hand the vote to the W. C. T., who shall announce the same.

33. In voting by yeas and nays, all present in regular standing in the Lodge must vote, unless excused by the Lodge ; but no member shall vote who was not in the room at the time the question was put. A motion to excuse, shall be decided without debate.

FILLING BLANKS.

34. When any blank is to be filled by the names of persons, a vote shall be taken on the names in the order of their nomination ; but when a blank is to be filled by any sum of money or time proposed, the question shall be first put on the largest sum, and the most remote time.

RECONSIDERATION AND REPEAL.

35. A question may be reconsidered any time during the session, or at the first regular session held thereafter ; but a motion for reconsideration, being once made and decided in the negative, shall not be renewed before the next regular session.

36. A motion to reconsider must be made and seconded by members who voted in the majority. No question shall be reconsidered more than once ; nor shall a vote to reconsider, be reconsidered. To reconsider a resolution, &c., the decision of which has officially passed out of the Lodge, shall not be in order.

37. A motion to repeal or rescind a resolution, shall be offered in writing, and announced at a regular session, two weeks before action shall be taken on the same ; and shall only be in order when the motion to reconsider is no longer available.

COMMITTEES AND THEIR REPORTS.

38. The first one named in the appointment of a Committee shall be Chairman of the same, and shall cal the Committee together at such time and place as he may select; but when thus convened, any Committee may elect its own Chairman and Secretary.

39. All reports of Committees, except reports of progress, shall be made in writing, and signed by a majority.

40. When a majority's report is followed by a report from the minority of a Committee, the former, after being read, shall lie upon the table until the latter is presented; after which, on motion, either may be considered.

41. When a report has been read, it shall be considered as properly before the Lodge, without a motion to accept.

BY-LAWS.

PREAMBLE.

We, the members of this Lodge, desirous of forming an organization to shield us from the evils of intemperance, afford mutual assistance in case of adversity, and elevate our character as citizens, do pledge ourselves to be governed by the foregoing Constitution, and the following By-Laws:—

1. A regular meeting of this Lodge shall be held on ....evening of each week or fortnight.

2. The hour of meeting shall be ...... o'clock, from the first of October to the first of April, and ...... o'clock, from the first of April to the first of October. The Lodge shall close punctually at ten o'clock, unless two-thirds of of the members present vote to the contrary

FINES, PENALTIES, AND PRIVILEGES.
FOR ABSENCE.

3. The Officers of this Lodge, for absence at the time of calling the roll at any regular meeting, shall be fined as follows, viz. :—Worthy Chief Templar, Worthy Vice Templar, Secretary, Financier, Marshal, each.... cents; all other officers .... cents.

ABSENCE OF BOOKS.

4. For neglecting to have the books of the Lodge present at any regular meeting, a fine of ....cents shall be imposed for each neglect.

REFUSING TO WATCH.

5. Members who shall refuse to watch with the sick on the nights which fall to them, as directed in No. 21 of these By Laws, when notified of the fact by the Committee for the sick, shall pay a fine of .... for each night of

refusal, unless they furnish a substitute, or give the Com·
mittee such good reasons as will cause them to be excused
by the Lodge.

FINES—HOW TO BE SETTLED.

6. All fines thus imposed, if not settled at the time, shall
be charged by the F. to the officer or member from whom
due, and shall stand against said officer or member as regul·
ar dues, and must be liquidated to entitle him to the pass·
word and the privilege of voting.

EXCUSES.

7. Sickness, or absence from the place on necessary busi·
ness, shall be the only reasons which can be accepted by
the Chair for the non-payment of fines. No other excuse
shall be granted, except by a regular motion, and a vote of
the Lodge.

TATTLING MEMBERS.

8. Any member of this Lodge found guilty of divulging
the name of another who may speak or vote against a candidate for initiation, or if any member make public any of
the business or transactions of the Lodge, said member shall
be fined, suspended, or expelled, as the Lodge may direct;
and, if fined, the fine shall in no case be less than.........
dollars.

9. Any member of this Lodge who shall reply to, or notice
any question regarding the business, passwords, signs, or
other private works of the Order, from any one not a mem·
ber in good standing, and tending to expose matters which
should be confined to this Lodge, shall be considered un·
worthy of membership, and may be expelled by a vote of
the Lodge.

DECORUM.

10. Any member who shall, in this Lodge, use profane or
objectionable and improper language, or refuse to obey the
commands of the Chair, when called to order, or make dis·
respectful expressions towards the officers or members of

this Lodge, shall oe subject to a fine for each offence, not
exceeding .... dollars, or to expulsion, as the Lodge
may direct.

CONDUCT.

11. Any member who shall become addicted to any vicious
or immoral habits, which will injure himself or his family,
and disgrace this Order, shall be expelled.

FEES AND DUES.—INITIATION.

12. The Initiation Fee of this Lodge shall be ...... cents
for each brother, and ...... cents for each sister.

DUES.

13. Every member of this Lodge shall pay in advance into
the general fund .... cents weekly, monthly, or quarterly,
to defray the necessary expenses of this Lodge.

CARDS.

14. Members of the Order may be admitted as members
of this Lodge by Card, on payment of ...... cents by brothers, and ...... cents by sisters.

15. Members wishing a Card of Clearance from the Lodge
are entitled to it if clear upon the book of the Financier,
on payment of ...... cents by brothers, and ...... cents
by sisters.

FUNDS.—HOW APPROPRIATED.

16. The funds of this Lodge shall be used for defraying
the necessary expenses of this Lodge, and to pay the taxes
levied by the Grand Lodge.

17. No money shall be appropriated, or used for other
purposes than those mentioned in No. 16 of these By-Laws,
unless, two-thirds of all the members present at a regular
meeting of this Lodge vote to do so.

COMMITTEES.

18. All Committees, unless otherwise ordered, shall consist of three members.

19. The W. C. T., shall, on the night of his installation, appoint the following Standing Committees for his term :—
A Committee on Finance.
A Committee on the Care of the Sick.
A Room Committee.

FINANCE COMMITTEE—DUTIES OF

20. The duties of the Finance Committee are to examine and audit bills and accounts presented to this Lodge for payment, as also the Reports and accounts of the Treasurer and Financier; and to report, at the next meeting after their appointment, the state of the Finances, detailing the amount due by each member.

COMMITTEE ON THE CARE OF THE SICK—DUTIES OF

21. The Committee on the care of the sick shall consist of three brothers and three sisters. It shall be the duty of this Committee to visit the sick, within twenty-four hours of being apprized of a member's sickness; they shall render to the brother or sister every assistance which will appear to them called for; give aid and comfort to the patient; and, if watches are required, they shall notify two members for each night, calling upon them in the order in which they stand upon the roll of the Lodge, the Committee serving themselves in their regular order. Fines for non-compliance with the provisions of this section, are to be strictly enforced. Sec. No. 5.

ROOM COMMITTEE—DUTIES OF.

22. This Committee are to see that the Room and the Regalia are always in readiness for meeting, and perform such other duties as the Lodge may require.

MISCELLANEOUS SECTIONS.

23. Suspended members shall pay the whole sum due from them up to the time of re-instatement.

ELECTIONS.

24. No Officer shall be declared elected, who has not re ceived a majority of all the legal votes cast.

TRUSTEES.

25. This Lodge shall elect three Trustees at the last reg- ular meeting in October, in each year, who shall transact all the legal business for the Lodge.

TREASURER.

26. The amount of the bond of the Treasurer of this Lodge shall be . ... dollars, but this amount may be at any time increased by a vote of the Lodge.

DEGREE MEETINGS.

27. The Degree Meetings of this Lodge shall be held at the usual hour, on the evening of the .... in each month.

AMENDMENTS.

28. No part of these By-Laws, shall be repealed, altered, or anulled, unless a notice to that effect be presented in writing to the Lodge, which shall lie over for two weeks before action shall be had thereon, when, if two-thirds of the members present vote in favor of the amendment, it shall be adopted.

APPENDIX.

FORMS.

Application for a Worthy Grand Lodge Charter. See W. G. L. Constitution, Art. 1.

To Brother ...., M. W. G. Secretary,

The undersigned, being Past or Present Chiefs of Lodges, No. 1, No. 2, No. 3, &c., of British Templars, in the ....of ....,
respectfully petition the M. W. Grand Lodge to grant a Charter to open a W. Grand Lodge to be called " The Worthy Grand Lodge of the British Templars of ....; " and we pledge ourselves individually and collectively to be governed by the rules, ceremonies, and usages of " British Templars."

Enclosed is the W. Grand Charter Fee, $12.

.....................P. W. C., No. 1.
.....................W. C. T., No. 2.
&c. &c. &c.

Application for a Primary Lodge Charter. See W. G. L. Constitution, Art. 2, and Gen. R. 28, 29, 31.

To the Worthy Grand Lodge of the British Templars of...........

We, the undersigned, inhabitants of ...., believing the " British Templars " well calculated to extend the blessings of Total Abstinence, and promote the general welfare of mankind, respectfully petition the Worthy Grand Lodge of ...., to grant us a Charter to open a Lodge, to be called " ....Primary Lodge, No......, of British Templars," to be located in..................., County of ...., and under your jurisdiction. We pledge ourselves to be governed by the rules and usages of the Order.

Enclosed is the Charter Fee, $8.

[For Juvenile Charter use the above Form, changing " inhabitants" into *youths*—" Primary " into *Juvenile*—" your jurisdiction " into *the jurisdiction of* ....*Primary Lodge, No......*; and " $8 " into $1.]

Form of Certificate and Recommendation of Provincial Deputy. See W. G. L. Con., Art. 8.

To the Worthy Grand Chief Templar of ....

    This is to certify that Brother .... has this evening, ... been duly elected to the office of Provincial Deputy for .... Lodge, No......... ; and we beg leave to recommend him as a fit and proper person to be commissioned to hold that important position.

    In witness whereof, we cause this to be signed by our W. C. T. and Secretary, and the seal of our Lodge to be attached.

    [L.S.]   ...., W. C. T.

                                        ...., Sec'y.

Form of Charge.

To ....Lodge, No......, British Templars :

    I hereby charge Brother (or Sister) ...., a member of this Lodge, with having violated Article III of our Constitution (or No. ...... of our By Laws, or his or her obligation, as the case may be,) on ...... day of ...., 18..., at .... ; and I pray that a Committee of Investigation may be appointed.   ....

                                      Member of Lodge No...

Dated this ...... day of ...., 18...

Form of Summons. See P. L. Con., Sec. 3, 4, Art. 16.

To Brother (or Sister) ...., a member of ....Lodge, No...... British Templars :

    You are hereby notified to appear before the undersigned Committee, at (or in) ...., on the ...... day of ...., 18..., at ...... o'clock, ... m., and answer to the charge annexed to this summons. In case you fail to appear, you will be reported to the Lodge as guilty of contempt, and will incur expulsion therefrom, unless you can render a satisfactory excuse.

Dated this .... day of ...., 18...   ....⎫ Committee.

[NOTE.—This summons should be served personally on the accused at least one week before trial, or left at the Post Office or at his last place of residence, at least ten days previous to the day of hearing. The accuser should also be notified of the time and place of meeting, that he may produce his evidence to sustain the charge.]

Form of Notification to a Witness.

To ....:

You are hereby notified (or requested, to a person not a member of the Order,) to meet the undersigned Committee at (or in) ...., on the ...... day of ...., 18..., at ...... o'clock, ... m., to testify what you know concerning the validity of the grounds for the charge against ...., a member of .... Lodge, No ......, British Templars.

Dated this ...... day of   .... ⎞
......., 18...   .... ⎬ Committee.
                              .... ⎠

Form of Credential of Representative.

To the Officers and Members of the W. Grand Lodge :

This is to certify that Brother (or Sister) ...., W. C. T., (W. V. T., or P. W. C., or P. W. V.) has been duly elected to represent ....Lodge, No ......, in the W. Grand Lodge of ...., until February next, unless meantime disqualified.

  [Seal.]   ...., W. C. T.
  [Date.]   ...., Secy.

Form of Certificate of Financier, to be given on payment of Dues.

                          ....Lodge, No......, British Templars.

This certifies that Brother (or Sister) ...., has paid all dues and charges against ...... up to..............

Dated this...... day of .... 18...

                        ...., Financier.

Form of Order on Treasurer.

No......, ...Lodge, No..., British Templars.

                            ...., 18...

Brother (or Sister) ...., Treasurer :

     Pay to ...., or order, the sum of ....dollars and ...... cents, for ....; as voted by the Lodge.

                        ...., W. C. T.
  $......   ...., Secy.

Form of Proposition for Membership.

.........................., 18...

Members of ....Lodge, No ..., British Templars.

I recommend, as worthy to become a member of this Lodge,
M..................., of........................

.... } Referees.　..........................
....   Member of Lodge No....

Form of Treasurer's Bond.

KNOW ALL MEN BY THESE PRESENTS, That we, ..., and ....
of ...., County of........., ..., are held and firmly bound unto
.... W. C. T. of .... Lodge, No. ..., located in ...., and
...., W. V. T., and ...., P. W. C. of the same Lodge, in trust
for said Lodge, in the penal sum of ....dollars, good and lawful
money of ...., to be paid to the said ...., ..., and ....,
their heirs, executors, administrators, and assigns, in trust, as aforesaid ; to which payment well and truly to be made, we do bind ourselves, our heirs, executors, and administrators, firmly by these presents. Sealed with our seals, and dated this ...... day of ...., A. D.
18... .

THE CONDITION OF THIS OBLIGATION is that—Whereas the said ....
has been duly elected Treasurer of the said Lodge, for the quarter
commencing on the first day of ...., A. D. 18.... ; now if the said
.... sha l well and faithfully perform the duties of said office, pay
all orders legally drawn on ......, when in funds ; and at the end of ......
term, account for, and pay over to .... successor in office, all moneys
that may have come into ...... hands ; then this Ob igation to be void,
else to remain in full force.

Witness our hands and seals, the day and year aforesaid.

.... [L. S.]
Signed, sealed, and delivered　.......................... [L. S.]
in the presence of

....
....

www.ingramcontent.com/pod-product-compliance
Lightning Source LLC
Chambersburg PA
CBHW022008190326
41519CB00010B/1434